The Kitchen Witches

by Caroline Smith

A SAMUEL FRENCH ACTING EDITION

SAMUEL FRENCH

FOUNDED 1830

SAMUELFRENCH.COM

ISBN 978-0-573-63286-0   Printed in U.S.A.   #12996

MUSIC USE NOTE

Licensees are solely responsible for obtaining formal written permission from copyright owners to use copyrighted music in the performance of this play and are strongly cautioned to do so. If no such permission is obtained by the licensee, then the licensee must use only original music that the licensee owns and controls. Licensees are solely responsible and liable for all music clearances and shall indemnify the copyright owners of the play and their licensing agent, Samuel French, Inc., against any costs, expenses, losses and liabilities arising from the use of music by licensees.

IMPORTANT BILLING AND CREDIT REQUIREMENTS

All producers of *THE KITCHEN WITCHES must* give credit to the Author of the Play in all programs distributed in connection with performances of the Play, and in all instances in which the title of the Play appears for the purposes of advertising, publicizing or otherwise exploiting the Play and/ or a production. The name of the Author *must* appear on a separate line on which no other name appears, immediately following the title and *must* appear in size of type not less than fifty percent of the size of the title type.

THE KITCHEN WITCHES premiered at the Stirling Festival Theatre in Stirling, Ontario on June 11, 2003. The performance featured sets by Franklin G. Stapley, costumes by Alice Fleming, lighting by Renée Brode, set painting by Lise Lindenberg and Perry Poupore, props by Donna Moorman, "Witches Jingle" by Michael Barber. The Production Stage Manager was Marilyn Lawrie. The cast was as follows:

DOLLY BIDDLE	Diane Fabian
STEPHEN BIDDLE	Ken MacDougall
ISOBEL (IZZY) LOMAX	Barbara Wheeldon
ROB THE CAMERA GUY	Rob Middleton

THE KITCHEN WITCHES was the winner of the 2005 Samuel French Canadian Playwrights Competition

CHARACTERS

DOLLY BIDDLE - A 50ish little cherub of a woman, prone to overweight but always going at top speed. She indulges herself with anything life has to offer whenever possible - even if it's not good for her - and her creative imagination knows no bounds. She is intensely proud of her son, Stephen, loves to dispense advice along with recipes for cabbage rolls and borscht and hates Isobel Lomax with an intensity usually reserved for detonating nuclear devices.

STEPHEN BIDDLE - A nervous, prematurely balding, but decent young man who actually enjoys producing low-budget cable TV shows, even when it's his mom who's the star. He is 30ish, bright and capable, if somewhat shy, but always reluctant to confront Dolly on her many shortcomings. He's not a fighter - he'd rather be a lover, but nobody's asked him yet.

ISOBEL LOMAX - Thinks Martha Stewart could learn something about homemaking from her. She trained at the Cordon Bleu and enjoyed a successful career, including her own show, *Busy Izzy*. Isobel likes people to think she has a much classier background than reality supports, and always wears the correct accessories. At heart, she is a bright, funny, and articulate woman who has come to terms with the choices she made early in life.

ROB THE CAMERA GUY (or Chick) - Can be played by an ASM or actual production assistant. The production assistant from the "Getting Our Kids Off the Street" program. Rob (Robbie/Roberta/ or use whatever name you choose!) tends to dress in a somewhat "Goth" fashion - possibly with tattoos and multiple piercings - Stephen is a little afraid of him/her. He/she cleans up the sets, resets props, carries the portable camera around during the show and is generally extremely efficient and precise. He/she is probably the most sensible person in the show.

PRODUCTION NOTES

The whole show takes place in a television studio, supposedly broadcast live with a studio audience. The show can be played with a video element or without.

If budget and tech capabilities allow, monitors can be placed so that the "studio audience" can see what the viewing audience at home can see. However, in the original production, we decided not to use monitors, since we felt it was more important for the audience to watch the action on stage. We also decided not to use stationary "studio cameras" since they interfered with audience sight-lines. We didn't miss them. The show is very prop-heavy and approximately $20 of food is used per show.

The character of "Rob" (or in case of a female, Roberta) can be played by an actor or - since he has only one line and his role is to carry around the shoulder camera and clear and re-set each scene—by an ASM.

Stephen has a live microphone at his podium - if budget allows, he should also have a small monitor.

Please note that all local references may be changed to the specific locations, sponsors etc. of the producing theatre.

ACT ONE

*(A rather seedy cooking-show set with a central counter and oven, fridge, etc. at upstage. Offstage right is a door leading to **DOLLY**'s dressing room, marked with a large "1" and a removable sign in a holder, saying "MS. BIDDLE." There is another dressing room on stage left, marked "2", but the name holder is empty. A third door leads to the rest of the TV station.)*

*(A young **GUY (ROB THE CAMERA GUY)** wearing blacks and a baseball hat is holding a shoulder-mount camera. A **MAN (STEPHEN)** in his 30's, wearing a somewhat-rumpled suit, enters and speaks to the "studio audience". He is a little uneasy about this – he really doesn't like public speaking.)*

STEPHEN. Good afternoon everyone, and welcome to *Baking with Babcha.* How are you all doing today? *(ad lib)* Good. Now – how many of you have ever been to a live TV show before? *(ad lib)* Okay, for you first-timers, let me tell you a little about what's going to happen here today. The show is *live,* which means that anything – and I mean anything - can happen, and thanks to the generosity of your Community Service Station, Cable Access Four, and our sponsors, the Stirling Creamery, Duke's Bait and Tackle Shop, and Wendy's Wicker World, the show will be instantly sent out over the airwaves and seen by...dozens of people. Anyway...

My name is Stephen Biddle, and I am *Baking with Babcha*'s producer and director. And this is Rob, our Audio-Visual Co-op student from the excellent "Getting Our Kids off the Street" program. It's our job to make sure that the show starts and ends on time and in between, see that you all have a lot of fun, right Rob?

(**ROB** *gives a bored "thumbs up".*)

STEPHEN. It's nice to see a couple of familiar faces here today...hello there, Mrs. Hutchinson – how's the rash? Good...And there's good old George... George? *(Over-enunciate, George is hard of hearing.)* Babcha wanted me to let you know she got your letter – *(He holds up a coloured piece of paper.)* and she thought your idea for using Babcha's Chocolate Syrup was really interesting. Unfortunately, health regulations forbid us from having Babcha, uh - *(He reads:)* "dip you in it from head to toe" as you suggest...you are not a well man, George.

(**ROB** *holds up one finger, indicating one minute to air...*)

Excuse me, folks –Rob is letting me know that we'll be live in just one minute – be right back...
(He crosses to the dressing room door and knocks.)
One minute, Babcha!

DOLLY. *(offstage)* Hokey dokey!

STEPHEN. *(putting on his headset)* Okay. Since today is our very last show, how about we bring Babcha on with the biggest round of applause ever! Just watch the sign and when it lights up, give it everything you've got. *(speaking through the headset to the unseen camera man at the back of the house)* Ready on Camera One, Lenny? Great. Have fun everyone! *(knocking on stage right door)* Fifteen seconds, Babcha! Have a great show!

DOLLY. *(from offstage, in thick Ukrainian accent)* Are they good audience?

STEPHEN. They're going to be a great audience, Babcha – best we've ever had!

DOLLY. Stephen, did you check props...

STEPHEN. You know I always check the props...

DOLLY. Did you check mail...

STEPHEN. Ma! Five seconds! I gotta go!!!

DOLLY. So go already, vot's keeping you?

STEPHEN. In … three… two… Cue music!

(A bouncy polka starts.)

(on microphone, over the music) Your Community Service Station, Cable Access Four, is proud to present the final live broadcast of… *Baking With Babcha*!

(The applause sign lights up and **DOLLY BIDDLE***, in somewhat tacky Ukrainian Grandma dress, emerges from her dressing room. She is, quite simply, a human dynamo. She crosses downstage, addressing the audience.)*

DOLLY. Hello, dears! Oh, so nice to see you today! Hello, Mrs. H, nice to see you not scratching - looking good! Hello, Georgie – Georgie - "dip me in chocolate!"- you are bad boy! *Bad* boy! *(She winks seductively.)* I speak to you after show, come to dressing room. Hoi! How is everyone today? Oh, so good, so good! And all you peoples watching at home, hello dears! Hello Elm Street United Ladies Bridge Club - Hello Mabel and Gladys at the Knitting Nook! *(She pronounces the "k" in "knitting" and the invisible "k" in "nook".)* Is so nice to have so many friends…Ah!! – but did you hear sad introduction? Yes, what my boy say is true – today is last *Baking with Babcha* show. Ya! After today, no more Babcha cabbage roll. No more Babcha borscht. No more Babcha. Is tragic, like Russian play.

And you know what is replacing *Baking With Babcha*? Eh? Eh? *Charlie's Chess Chat.* What kinda show is that? I got a better show to put on air – *Watching Grass Grow*. Is more exciting…Bolsheviks who run TV station, I tell you, they don't know nothing…

*(***STEPHEN*** is frantically signaling* **DOLLY** *to get on with the show.)*

Ah! My boy is trying to tell me to move on with show. Is good idea. Show only twenty minutes long! So. We get on with show. Have you met my boy, Stephen? No? Come here, Stephen, come…

STEPHEN. Babcha…

DOLLY. Is last show! What they gonna do, fire Babcha? Babcha is already fired!

*(She drags the reluctant **STEPHEN** into camera view.)*

Hello dears – say hello to Stephen. You know who is Stephen? Stephen is wonderful producer, wonderful director, and wonderful Babcha son! Say hello to peoples at home, dear.

STEPHEN. Hello peoples at home! Okay, Babcha…

DOLLY. Is hard-working, good-looking boy, yes? And you know vot? Babcha is so proud because Stephen is quit smoking! Such a good boy! How many days you quit now, Stephen?

STEPHEN. Four days, Ma.

DOLLY. Four days and no cancer stick, isn't that something? And you know what else?

STEPHEN. Oh, please don't…

DOLLY. Stephen is single! Can you believe, girls?

STEPHEN. Okay, that's enough, Babcha…

DOLLY. So he got no job now and hair is getting little thin, but…girls at home - you write letter to Babcha and maybe I make blind date, eh?

STEPHEN. Ma!

DOLLY. What?

STEPHEN. Back to the show?

DOLLY. Hey, this is show!

*(**STEPHEN** starts to speak…)*

Okay, okay, I get on with show!

*(**STEPHEN** returns to **ROB** at the camera.)*

I tell you, that boy is like a teepee and a wigwam… two tents! *("Too tense"…she laughs at her own joke, then abruptly slaps the counter and gets down to business.)* Okay! So today is last show, I am cooking special Last Ukrainian Supper. So on go the apron!

STEPHEN. *(on microphone)* Today's apron has been generously donated by...*(He reads a small business card.)* Cindy's Cellar of Sin...? What the...?

DOLLY. Stephen dear, apron donated from Dollar Store was okay if you like that kinda thing, but is last show and Babcha wants to go out with bang...

(She puts on "naked lady" apron.)

Bang! You like? Georgie, dear, don't look too close, pacemaker is not set for va-va-va-voom! Okay, now apron is on, what is first thing we do before we cook? We wash our hands! Okay, everybodys...let's all wash our hands...everybodys watching at home...okay, good! So. Last Ukrainian Supper. We make pyrohy *(pronounced* "pee-ro-heh*")* ...okay. You Canadians say "perogies"...is wrong, wrong, wrong!! Is insult. Every time you say "perogies", a Ukrainian grandmother dies. Is true! So say with me...pee-ro-*heh!* Pee-ro-*heh!* Good. Okay! Then, we make Ukrainian Rhum Baba... Poppy Seed Rum Cake! *(She pulls a mickey of rum from under the counter.)*

STEPHEN. *(off mic)* No...

DOLLY. Always use best ingredients...Babcha must taste rum for quality...

*(**STEPHEN** sneaks in under the camera line to take away the bottle; **DOLLY** pours a large shot, sips it...)*

Hmmm...I think is okay...*(...then downs the whole glass)* Is definitely okay! Hoo boy!!

*(**STEPHEN** sneaks the bottle off the counter, takes it back to the podium.)*

So. First make the borscht. In pot, we have ready, nice, beef stock. First we chop one big onion, sweet like lover's kiss; six pretty beets red like little children's cheeks, one nice carrot, long like...oh, boy! Okay, not too long.

(She chops off the end of the carrot.)

DOLLY. And now we chop, and we answer Babcha's mail. Stephen, we have letter?

STEPHEN. *(on mic)* Yes, we do, Babcha! This is from Jane in Belleville. She writes, "Dear Babcha, I have been watching you since the other Cable Four cooking show..." Uh, I'm sorry, Babcha, that's the wrong letter...

DOLLY. *(She has visibly stiffened.)* No, no, Stephen dear. What is in letter?

STEPHEN. It's nothing, Babcha...

DOLLY. *(threateningly)* Read letter.

STEPHEN. Uh... okay. "Dear Babcha, I have been watching you since the other Cable Four cooking show was cancelled last month. I was wondering, do you know Isobel Lomax, the hostess of *Busy Izzy* and if so, can you get me her recipe for Steak and Kidney Pie? Yours sincerely, Jane from Belleville"

DOLLY. *(smiling dangerously into the camera)* Hello Jane dear! Of course I know that person you mention. But you sound like nice lady, so I do nice thing. I don't get you recipe for Snake and Pygmy pie. I tell you reasons. Isobel Lomax is terrible cook, terrible TV host, terrible person....

STEPHEN. Okay, Babcha! It's time to take a little break and show the viewers at home our Community Service Announcements!

(Polka music fades up.)

DOLLY. Oh, boy! Time goes so fast on last show! Okay - you watch announcements, nice peoples, then come right back for rest of Last Ukrainian Supper. Okay! Bye – bye!

(The music stops and everyone relaxes.)

STEPHEN. We're clear. I've got to pick up the sponsor lists for the next segment. Rob, you're temporarily in charge –give Babcha the countdown after the community service announcements, okay?

(STEPHEN exits. As soon as he's gone, DOLLY reaches into her pocket and pulls out a small flask.)

DOLLY. Time to celebrate last show!

(She beckons ROB to come over and pours him a glass.)

Now everyone, we make this our little secret. What Stephen don't know won't hurt him, yes?

ISOBEL. *(from the audience)* I really have had enough of this.

(ISOBEL starts to make her way up onto the stage.)

DOLLY. Who is…*(She gasps.)* Isobel Lomax!

ISOBEL. How nice of you to remember me after all these years.

DOLLY. What on earth are you doing here?

ISOBEL. Over the past few weeks I have been watching this…*show.* I thought it time I came down in person and let you know I have had enough of this constant slander. Dolly Biddle, you have publicly insulted me for the last time. You can expect a call from my lawyer on Monday.

DOLLY. Go ahead! I never said a word on this show that wasn't true!

ISOBEL. Other than pretending to be something you're not.

DOLLY. What do you mean by that?

(ROB is holding up five fingers, then four…three… two…)

ISOBEL. You're about to go live again, dear…Does your viewing audience know that "Babcha from Ukraine" is really Dorothy Biddle from Sudbury?

DOLLY. *(dropping the accent)* No! And they never will!

(ROB indicates "You're on".)

Hello again, nice peoples…

ISOBEL. Hello, folks – Busy Izzy here! Sharing a kitchen with my good friend Dolly Biddle.

DOLLY. Dolly Biddle, who is that? I am Babcha!…

ISOBEL. Come on, Dolly, it's your last show - let the people see the real you.

DOLLY. *(through her teeth)* I warn you, Isobel...

ISOBEL. She used to be Dolly Plotznik, you know. Biddle is her married name....

DOLLY. At least I got married! At least I *had* a husband!

ISOBEL. Well, I *had* your husband more than you ever did!

DOLLY. Take that back!

ISOBEL. You know perfectly well I dated Larry Biddle first.

DOLLY. In your dreams! I was going steady with Larry long before you oozed onto the scene! Who did he take to the Senior Prom, huh?

ISOBEL. Who did he take to the Spring Social?

DOLLY. We got engaged in June of 1964!

ISOBEL. And broke up in August!

DOLLY. And married in December!

ISOBEL. Well, Larry may have married you, but I was the one who made him happy!

DOLLY. That man was never happy!

ISOBEL. How could he be, living with you? *(She points her "ring" hand.)*

DOLLY. What is that?

ISOBEL. What – this? *(And she holds up her hand, showing off a flashy ring.)*

DOLLY. That's...that's the Biddle family heirloom ring!

ISOBEL. Yep.

DOLLY. It was Larry's Great-Grandmother's!

ISOBEL. Yep.

DOLLY. How did...

ISOBEL. Larry gave it to me.

DOLLY. When?

ISOBEL. When we were dating.

DOLLY. He told me he lost it.

ISOBEL. Nope.

DOLLY. You…you must have stolen it…

ISOBEL. How dare you!

DOLLY. That ring should be mine!

ISOBEL. You can pry this from my cold, dead hand!

DOLLY. *(picking up her chopping knife)* Fine by me!

STEPHEN. *(re-entering)* Stop!!!

(They do.)

What the hell is going on here?

DOLLY.

ISOBEL.

This woman barged in here, interrupted my show and tore my blouse tried to take it over! I know she did it on purpose just to make me look bad *(etc.)*

Stephen? My name is Isobel Lomax. After listening to your mother bad-mouth me for years I decided to give her a taste of her own medicine *(etc.)*

STEPHEN. Everybody…time out!

(They quiet.)

Sorry folks. Babcha – please go back to your Borscht. And Miss Lomax, if you would just step over here out of camera range…

ISOBEL. Make me.

STEPHEN. What?

ISOBEL. Call me Miss Bird's Eye, I'm frozen to the spot!

(pause)

DOLLY. Well? What are you waiting for? Drag her out!

STEPHEN. I…Ma, you know I have a bad back…

DOLLY/ISOBEL. Just like his father.

STEPHEN. Look, can't you two just shake hands and call it a day?

DOLLY. You want me to shake hands with the woman who broke up your parent's marriage?

ISOBEL. Your marriage was over before it started. It never should have happened.

DOLLY. But it did, didn't it!

ISOBEL. He only married you because I said no.

DOLLY. Excuse me?

ISOBEL. You know perfectly well that Larry Biddle asked me to marry him before he asked you! But it was the sixties - I didn't want to settle down. I was too busy burning my bra!

DOLLY. I'm surprised something that small could catch fire! (*Or if Isobel is full-chested: "With all that Kleenex in there, it must have burned for a week!"*)

STEPHEN. Ladies…

ISOBEL. You know, Larry didn't even like your cooking!

DOLLY. Now, that is an outright lie!

ISOBEL. (*slowly and smugly*) He told me so the night he died.

STEPHEN. Wait a minute. You know something about the night my father died?

ISOBEL. Of course…

DOLLY. Stephen, dear – you don't need to hear this…

STEPHEN. All you told me was he had a heart attack.

DOLLY. You were only six when he died, Stephen. How do you tell a six year-old that his daddy was in a No-Tell Motel getting busy with Izzy?

STEPHEN. You mean – he died while you were…

ISOBEL. Yep. It wasn't so much a heart attack as a coronary orgasm.

STEPHEN. I think I'm gonna throw up.

DOLLY. The shame of it all. We had to arrange a closed coffin.

ISOBEL. Yeah. They couldn't get the smile off his face.

(**ROB** *is indicating that there's one minute left.*)

STEPHEN. Wrap it up, ladies…

DOLLY. (*in her Ukrainian accent*) Well, it's been so nice sharing time with you each week, peoples, and Babcha is so sorry to say goodbye. So– everybodys…remember to eat good, enjoy life and most important…wash your hands!

STEPHEN. Stay tuned for *Macramé with Sister Mary Mildred*, coming up next on Cable Access Four.

DOLLY. This is Babcha…

ISOBEL. *(butting into the camera)* And Busy Izzy!

DOLLY. Saying goodbye!

ISOBEL. And good cooking!

(They wave into the camera as the polka jingle plays them out.)

STEPHEN. We're clear.

DOLLY. Goodbye George, dear – don't forget to drop me a line once in a while. Good-bye, Mrs. H.!

(She waves goodbye until the studio audience is "gone." **ROB** *exits, returning with tubs and clearing away the tops of the counters.)*

STEPHEN. Well, that was one way to leave show business.

ISOBEL. Despite the unfortunate circumstances - Stephen, it was nice meeting you.

(A red light on the wall is blinking on and off. **ROB** *whistles to get* **STEPHEN** *'s attention then continues clearing the set.)*

STEPHEN. Excuse me.

ISOBEL. It seems that my work here is done. My lawyer will be in touch.

STEPHEN. *(taking the phone from* **ROB***)* Hello?

DOLLY. You just had to mess things up for me one more time, didn't you. Just couldn't ever let me have the last word.

ISOBEL. Funny - in my recollection, you always had the last word, every single time. But here is my very last word to you – Goodbye!

(She starts to exit.)

STEPHEN. Just a minute, Miss Lomax – it's for you.

ISOBEL. Me? Who would be calling me here?

DOLLY. Satan. He wants to know when you'll be home.

ISOBEL. *(taking the phone)* Hello?

STEPHEN. Okay, Ma. Let's start packing this stuff up. *(He starts taking down the* Baking With Babcha *sign.)*

DOLLY. Stephen dear, about your dad...

STEPHEN. I'll drive you home. We'll talk about it later...

ISOBEL. Really! How nice of you to say that. Thank you, dear, I wish you all the best as well. *(hangs up)* Well! That was one of my fans, calling to say how much they enjoyed my show today.

DOLLY. Your show?! Well of all the...

ISOBEL. Excuse me, dear, there seems to be another call... *(picks up receiver)* Hello, it's Busy Izzy! ...Oh, yes. Of course...

(holds the receiver out to DOLLY*)*

It's for you.

*(*DOLLY *switches to her Babcha accent:)*

DOLLY. Hello? Oh, hello, girls! Stephen!

(He looks up from his cleaning.)

It's the Elm Street United Ladies Bridge Club.

(back into receiver) Really? You did? Did we have...what? *(covers the receiver)* They say that was the funniest show they've ever seen, they loved it and did we have someone write the script or did we improvise?

STEPHEN. Tell them...tell them I wrote it.

DOLLY. We improvised...Oh, yes, that was all made up! Well, thank you so much, girls...yes. You too! Bye bye.

(She hangs up. The light instantly comes on again.)

There's another call.

STEPHEN. Here. Let me handle this. *(picks up receiver)* Stephen Biddle...Oh, Mr. Patterson! So nice of you to call...

ISOBEL. Is that Hugh Patterson?

DOLLY. Who?

STEPHEN. *(covering the receiver)* Ssshhh! *(back into phone)* You did? Really?

ISOBEL. Programming Executive Hugh Patterson, you dolt!

DOLLY. *(moving closer to **STEPHEN**)* Oh!

STEPHEN. Yes…And will you…All right - yes, of course, I'll tell them. No, thank you, sir. *(hangs up)*

DOLLY / ISOBEL. Well?

STEPHEN. Mr. Patterson says he loved the show today. Said it beat his favourite programs, Martha Stewart and Jerry Springer. He can't wait to see you again next week…

DOLLY. But I won't be on next week!

STEPHEN. Let me finish. He can't wait to see both of you again next week in this brilliant new show format. Then if next week is as good as this week, he'll make it part of the regular programming.

ISOBEL. You mean - he wants us on the air again?

DOLLY. Together?

STEPHEN. That's what he wants.

ISOBEL. Stephen, we can't share a show – within five minutes, one of us would be dead…

DOLLY. …And the other charged with murder! We've hated each other almost forty years!

STEPHEN. I think that's the idea.

ISOBEL. Well, it's a ridiculous idea. I have no intention of continuing to air my personal affairs in public. Besides, I've had a lot of other offers, you know…

DOLLY. Bull! You've had about as many offers as I've had, which is none. And as far as airing your personal affairs, you have *always* opened your big fat cakehole to anyone who would listen!

ISOBEL. That is an outright lie! I am an extremely private person!

DOLLY. Ha! You're about as private as a Kardashian's cleavage.

STEPHEN. All right! All right! If you both think this is such a bad idea, I will call Mr. Patterson and tell him that neither of you are willing to continue with the show.

DOLLY/ISOBEL. Fine!

STEPHEN. You can both retire and look forward to years of undisturbed peace and tranquility. Maybe even move into one of those nice retirement homes.

(The ladies are looking less sure of themselves.)

Endless hours of sitting quietly on the porch, learning macramé with Sister Mary Mildred...cups of tea and ham sandwiches on unbuttered white bread... Bedtime at 8:30. Unless...

DOLLY/ ISOBEL. What?

STEPHEN. Unless we do script the show.

DOLLY. What do you mean, dear?

STEPHEN. I will create dialogue that you will both follow precisely. We can make up things for you to say that are scandalous and outrageous enough to keep the fans happy, but you won't have to air your own stories. What do you say?

DOLLY. *(after a long pause)* No way I'd share my dressing room with her.

STEPHEN. I'll get you separate dressing rooms. Ladies – it seems to me that we don't have much to lose. I know I don't. So what do you say?

DOLLY / ISOBEL. Let's try it. / Count me in.

STEPHEN. Great! I'll start a script outline and get the ball rolling...We'll need a new name...

ISOBEL. The Izzy and Dolly Show!

DOLLY. You mean the Dolly and Izzy show.

ISOBEL. Why should you get first billing?

DOLLY. It's always alphabetical.

ISOBEL. Or age before beauty!

DOLLY. Ha! You're older than I am!

ISOBEL. Since when?

DOLLY. Since God said, "Let there be light," and you threw the switch!

STEPHEN. I think I have it! How about…*The Kitchen Witches*!

(a pause)

ISOBEL. What are you implying?

DOLLY. Oh, I don't think you can describe me as a witch, Stephen…

ISOBEL. Unless you spell it with a 'B', Stephen.

DOLLY. All right, that tears it! I will continue with the show, but I would appreciate it if you keep her as far away from me as possible until we are on the air! I will be in my dressing room!

(and she exits, slamming the door)

ISOBEL. Here is my card, Stephen. Call me with the details. Kitchen Witches, indeed…

(And she heads for the exit door just as **ROB** *comes in.)*

Get the hell out of my way!

(She exits.)

STEPHEN. Rob?

*(***STEPHEN*** *hands him some money.)*

Go get me a pack of Nicorette and a large bottle of Tylenol– it's gonna be a bumpy ride….

*(***ROB*** *puts the bottle of rum in* **STEPHEN***'s hand and exits as we fade to…)*

(blackout)

SCENE TWO

(Lights come up on **STEPHEN**, *who is pacing back and forth.)*

*(***ROB*** *enters and sets out the bowls of ingredients for the next two scenes.)*

STEPHEN. Rob, have you seen them yet?

*(***ROB*** *shakes his head and exits.)*

Damn. Nine a.m. sharp, I said. We have the studio for exactly one hour to rehearse, so be prompt, I said. Where the hell is the new sign…Rob! Rob!!

*(***ROB*** *carries in a sign which says "Kitchen Witches".)*

Beautiful! Now all we need are the witches …

ISOBEL. *(entering)* Good morning, Stephen! Isn't it a lovely day!

STEPHEN. Witch number one! Miss Lomax, where –

ISOBEL. Oh, just Isobel, dear. No need to be so formal.

STEPHEN. All right – Isobel – Have you seen Dolly?

ISOBEL. Who?

STEPHEN. Dolly Biddle. My mother. Your co-host.

ISOBEL. Oh, I almost forgot all about her. Isn't she here?

STEPHEN. No. *(He resumes pacing.)*

ISOBEL. Oh, well. I'm sure she'll be along, dear – don't get yourself so agitated! You know you'll just end up with an ulcer.

STEPHEN. I don't have room for another ulcer.

ISOBEL. Stephen dear – is that my name I see on dressing room…two?

STEPHEN. Yes?

ISOBEL. And Dolly's on dressing room…one?

STEPHEN. So?

ISOBEL. So why does she get the room closest to the set?

STEPHEN. What?

ISOBEL. Dear, dressing room one is clearly closer to the set.

STEPHEN. *(looking at the symmetrical dressing room doors)* Uh… it is?

ISOBEL. That wouldn't have anything to do with the little bit of nepotism going on here, would it…

STEPHEN. Nepotism?

ISOBEL. …You being her son and all. Of course, it's natural for a boy to want his mother to have the best of everything…

STEPHEN. I honestly never…

ISOBEL. …but I'm sure you don't want Mr. Patterson to know you're playing favourites this early in the game, do you?

STEPHEN. I've never played favourites in my life…

ISOBEL. She's not here yet, you say?

STEPHEN. No, but…

ISOBEL. *(switching the name signs on the dressing rooms)* Well, dear, back in the days of my youth, we had a tradition that the early bird had the first pick of whatever was being handed out. So if you don't mind, I'll just get my things sorted and I'll be back in a flash to start rehearsing! Ta-ta!

(She exits into "her" room.)

STEPHEN. Isobel…

DOLLY. *(offstage)* Yoo-hoo!

STEPHEN. Witch number two…

*(**DOLLY** enters carrying a small shopping bag. **ROB** is trotting along behind her, loaded with bags.)*

DOLLY. Good morning, Stephen! Isn't it a beautiful day!

STEPHEN. Where have you been? Rehearsal was supposed to start…

DOLLY. Oh, I just thought I'd pick up a few necessities. You know how I like everything nice and fresh…put those down on the counter, Rob dear. *(She hands a long, long grocery tape to **STEPHEN**.)* Here's the receipt, you can pay me back later…where's Isobel?

STEPHEN. In her dressing room.

DOLLY. Oh. Well, then, I'll just go powder my nose...

STEPHEN. Not there!

DOLLY. What?

STEPHEN. You're...in dressing room *two*.

DOLLY. Now, Stephen, you know I always have dressing room one. It's closer to the set. It's got better lighting. It's dressing room *ONE!*

STEPHEN. Ma, they're exactly the same...

DOLLY. I thought with my asthma, mild diabetes, and heart condition...

STEPHEN. You don't *have* a heart condition... *(firmly)* Ma, Isobel got here first, so it's her dressing room now!

DOLLY. Oh. *(Her lower lip is quivering.)* I see.

STEPHEN. What?

DOLLY. I'm your mother and you don't want to be accused of favouritism, so I'm going to get the short end of the stick. *(She starts to cry.)*

STEPHEN. Please don't, I beg you...

DOLLY. Ever since your father died and I was left to raise you alone, a poor helpless, defenseless widow...I've tried to do my best for you. I've never expected anything back in return. No! Not one little thing. Except a little consideration in my old age...a little kindness now and again...

STEPHEN. Are you done?

DOLLY. I'll just go quietly to my dressing room...the *far-away* dressing room...and rest for a few moments... take my medication and get my strength back...then I'll be ready to go on... *(She exits.)*

STEPHEN. Rob ?

*(**ROB** re-enters with a nicotine patch.)*

Patch me. Please patch me.

*(**ROB** sticks the patch on **STEPHEN**'s arm then goes back to changing the set.)*

ISOBEL. *(re-entering)* Okay, ready when you are…isn't Dolly here yet?

STEPHEN. Yes, she's …uh…just in her dressing room…

ISOBEL. …thinking up some fresh new ways of getting under my skin, I bet.

STEPHEN. Isobel, can't you try and make nice with her, just for today?

ISOBEL. Well…

STEPHEN. As a favour to me? Please?

ISOBEL. Oh… *(she smiles)* I suppose so. Just because you're so damn *cute!* You know, you're much more handsome than your father was.

STEPHEN. Am I? I don't remember him much - I know him mostly by photos.

ISOBEL. Larry - your Dad - wasn't much to look at, but he had a certain charm, a certain… *air* about him. Made him completely irresistible…

STEPHEN. Uh…

ISOBEL. Oh, I'm sorry. I keep forgetting that I'm the "other woman." Does that bother you?

STEPHEN. It's…a little weird.

ISOBEL. Then let's not discuss it. We'll keep this all on a professional basis. If there's something you'd like to know about your father, ask me. If not, we don't ever have to talk about it again. Deal?

STEPHEN. Deal. Thank you, Isobel.

ISOBEL. Now, Stephen. Are you just going to stand around chatting all day, or are we going to start rehearsal?

STEPHEN. Rehearsal. Right…I'll just go and see if Camille has finished her death scene.

(**STEPHEN** *crosses to dressing room 2 and knocks on the door*)

DOLLY. *(in a weak voice, offstage)* Yes?

STEPHEN. We're ready, Ma.

DOLLY. *(entering)* I was just finishing taking my medicine…

(**STEPHEN** *quickly steps into her dressing room and emerges with an empty package*)

STEPHEN. Since when are Hostess Twinkies medicine?

DOLLY. I need a little energy for rehearsal.

STEPHEN. Ma, you've got to stop snacking! Especially stuff like this.

DOLLY. You know me and my sweet tooth.

STEPHEN. And you know what the doctor said…

DOLLY. Oh, what does that old quack know? He still believes in applying leeches!

STEPHEN. You promised me…

DOLLY. All right! Don't get your knickers in a twist!

(*She crosses to* **ISOBEL.**)

Good morning, Isobel.

ISOBEL. Good morning, Dolly. What an attractive blouse.

DOLLY. Thank you. And I do like your… now, what would you call that?

ISOBEL. It is a chef's jacket.

DOLLY. A *chef's jacket.* Of course. Very practical.

ISOBEL. Thank you.

DOLLY. But then again, you never did care about being in fashion, did you.

ISOBEL. As you recall, I was always *ahead* of each fashion trend, which was better than being *behind* it like some people I could mention…

STEPHEN. All right, ladies, how about we just give each other a little space and focus on the audience, and the cameras, and the food! Now, you already know we're calling the show *The Kitchen Witches* and I've written a script that I think is pretty good…

(*As he's saying this,* **ISOBEL** *has moved the bowl of flour.*)

DOLLY. What do you think you're doing?

ISOBEL. The flour was in the wrong place.

DOLLY. Excuse me, dear, but it's in exactly the right place. First the flour, then the salt then the sugar…

(They start re-arranging things.)

ISOBEL. No, dear, one never puts the salt next to the sugar, far too easy to select the wrong one. *(re-arranging again)*

DOLLY. *(more re-arranging)* For you, maybe. I can tell the difference between salt and sugar.

ISOBEL. Are you implying that I can't? *(manic re-arranging of bowls)*

STEPHEN. Stop it! Both of you! Look. I know if we all put our energy together we can come up with something really, really special.

(ROB enters with two large Kitchen Witch dolls.)

See our cute little Kitchen Witch here? She's not happy when she's down here on the ground, bickering, is she? *(imitating the ladies)* "Where's the salt? Where's the sugar? You're stupid! No, you are!"…No! She wants to rise above it all and soar like an eagle!

DOLLY. Oh, Stephen, what a lovely image!

ISOBEL. I say it's hard to soar like an eagle when you work with a turkey.

DOLLY. Who are you calling a turkey, you scrawny-necked buzzard?

ISOBEL. I calls 'em as I sees 'em!

STEPHEN. *(almost in tears)* Ladies! Focus! Please, for the love of…Look. If you two want to be treated as professionals, it's time you started acting that way!

ISOBEL. I'm sorry, Stephen. Dolly, I do apologize for my uncalled-for remark.

DOLLY. Apology accepted.

ISOBEL. Go ahead.

DOLLY. Yes, go ahead, dear.

STEPHEN. *(a little surprised that they're finally listening)* All right! Now we have a lot to go over today, so the first thing we'll do is…

DOLLY. Decide what kind of aprons we should wear.

STEPHEN. No, we should…

ISOBEL. Oh, now I do agree with Dolly on that point. Appearance is so important.

DOLLY. TV personalities are trend-setters, so it's vital that we look our very best at all times. So I hope you don't mind, Izzy - I was in the kitchen supply warehouse the other day and couldn't resist picking up a couple of aprons for us.

(**STEPHEN** *has crossed to his podium and is downing Tylenol.*)

ISOBEL. If great minds don't think alike! I picked up a couple of aprons for us as well!

DOLLY. Isn't that sweet! Tell you what – I'll show you mine if you show me yours!

ISOBEL. Okay! On three – one, two, three!

(*The women pull aprons from the bags on the counter.* **ISOBEL***'s is a classic men's tuxedo tailored apron.* **DOLLY***'s is a Las Vegas sequined thing.*)

DOLLY / ISOBEL. What the hell is that? (*to* **STEPHEN**) I am not wearing that.

STEPHEN. Please. Just…one favour before I die. Could we maybe…*open* our scripts?!

DOLLY. Well, of course!

ISOBEL. Why didn't you say so?

DOLLY. My goodness, dear, you don't have to make such a fuss.

STEPHEN. (*calming himself*) Good. Good. Now. What we're going to be doing each week is focusing on recipes from one part of the world…

ISOBEL. You mean, like French cooking one week…

DOLLY. …Italian the next?

STEPHEN. Exactly. Terry's Travel is our show sponsor, so…

DOLLY. I could do all my accents! (*in "Swedish"*) Allo! Today ve are making Svedish meatballs …And we could wear different costumes and things!

ISOBEL. I am not going to wear any costumes!

STEPHEN. We don't have that much money in the budget, Ma...

ISOBEL. I've been meaning to mention this - would you two mind very much dropping this "Ma" business? I find it quite unprofessional.

DOLLY. Unprofessional...!

STEPHEN. No, no – Isobel is right. First-names for everyone, across the board. Is that okay with you - Dolly?

DOLLY. Well, of course, Stephen. But I resent being called unprofessional. I have always conducted myself in a completely professional manner. For example, before I touch any food, I always wash my hands thoroughly and remove all *hand jewelry. (She demonstrates by removing rings and watch.)*

ISOBEL. I wondered when you'd get to that. You know perfectly well that I also remove my jewelry before handling food – what bugs you is the fact that I still wear Larry's ring!

DOLLY. You have no right whatsoever to wear it.

ISOBEL. I have been wearing this for over thirty years.

DOLLY. That doesn't make it right.

STEPHEN. Isobel...Dolly...the script!

(Glaring at each other, the **WOMEN** *open their scripts.)*

Now, we'll play the new jingle, something like, "They'll keep you in stitches, the Kitchen Witches"...

ISOBEL / DOLLY. Isn't that clever! / Cute!

STEPHEN. I say, "Your Community Service Station, Cable Access Four, is proud to present the premiere broadcast of... *The Kitchen Witches!*" Then the camera pans down to the two of you standing behind the counter and...

(He points a "go" finger at them, indicating they're on.)

ISOBEL. *(reading)* "Good morning, everyone and welcome to the *Kitchen Witches* Show"...well, that's pretty bland.

DOLLY. Why does she get the first line?

STEPHEN. *(working hard to be patient)* I tossed a coin.

ISOBEL. Couldn't I say something more interesting, like… *(in a "wicked witch" voice)* "A witchy welcome to one and all!"

DOLLY. Oh, that *is* better, Stephen…

STEPHEN. All right, fine! Say that.

DOLLY. Although I think it would be stronger if we *both* said it!

STEPHEN. Great! You *both* say it. Let's start again!

(The ladies do nothing.)

What?

ISOBEL. We're waiting for you to cue us.

*(**STEPHEN** heaves a huge sigh – then cues them.)*

DOLLY / ISOBEL. "A witchy welcome to one and all!"

DOLLY. And we could cackle a little…

(And they do.)

ISOBEL. And how about if we had a cauldron here on the counter, kind of smoking…

DOLLY. Oo, yes!

STEPHEN. NO! No cauldrons! Remember, it's not a show about *witches*, it's a show about cooking and dishing some dirt.

ISOBEL. Right.

STEPHEN. Okay. We've said hello. It took 15 minutes, but we've said hello. Go on.

*(She waits for **STEPHEN** to cue her. He almost dislocates his arm in doing so.)*

DOLLY. "On today's show we're going to feature classic recipes from the old South …" Why the old South?

STEPHEN. Terry's Travel has a special on Carolina getaways, so I thought we'd tie it in.

DOLLY. Oh. "… recipes from the old South."

ISOBEL. "And speaking of old, did you know that Dolly doesn't have an enemy in the world? She's outlived them all."

(STEPHEN *chuckles. The* WOMEN *don't.*)

Stephen - is that supposed to be funny or argumentative?

STEPHEN. Uh – both, I thought...

ISOBEL. Oh.

(*She makes a note in her script.*)

All right...your turn...

DOLLY. Well, you look like a million. Every year of it..."

(STEPHEN *howls. The women look at him, stone-faced.*)

Stephen, dear. Did you write this all by yourself?

STEPHEN. (*sobering*) Well, I haven't had much time, you know...

ISOBEL. Maybe we should just ad-lib the opening bit...

STEPHEN. No! I think it's safer to stick to the script.

DOLLY. Yes. Give it a chance, Isobel!

ISOBEL. Here we go with the favouritism again! Doesn't matter what I say, the two of you will gang up on me and do whatever you want! I see the way this is going!

STEPHEN. Isobel...

DOLLY. Don't bother arguing with her. You might as well try to talk to a jackass.

ISOBEL. So now I'm a jackass?

DOLLY. If the horseshoe fits...

ISOBEL. All I'm saying is that it doesn't take a genius to know that this script smells worse than five-week old cabbage! Fix it or that's the last you'll see of Isobel Lomax!!!

(*She exits to the dressing room and slams the door.*)

DOLLY. Stephen, if you wish to discuss this further, I will be in my dressing room. That would be the aptly-named... number two! (*slams door*)

STEPHEN. (*after a pause*) Okay. That went pretty well.

(*blackout*)

SCENE THREE

(The broadcast of the first Kitchen Witches *show.* **STEPHEN** *is scurrying around, speaking into his headset.* **ROB** *is at the camera.)*

STEPHEN. Lenny, it's two minutes to air, are you trying to give me a heart attack? No, I know we're all working as hard as we can, Lenny, but I still need more light on the set...no, not on the floor, on the set...

(The light on the phone is flashing. **ROB** *picks it up and indicates to* **STEPHEN** *that it's for him.)*

What is it now...Hello? Mr. Patterson, how are you, sir! ...Oh, no, I wouldn't miss this for the world either, sir! Yes, we worked out the problem with the dressing rooms. Isobel is fine with her room being two-and-a-half inches narrower than Dolly's now that Isobel has the Tiffany reading lamp. And Dolly says she can live with the fact that Isobel's shower has more water pressure, because she's got the skinny mirror. No, I have no idea what a skinny mirror is...

*(***DOLLY** *emerges from her dressing room, wearing a dressing gown.)*

DOLLY. Stephen, darling...

STEPHEN. Just a minute, Mr. Patterson. What do you need, Ma?

DOLLY. Just wanted to wish you good show!

STEPHEN. Thanks...

DOLLY. Oh - and I know you didn't have any budget for costumes but being as today's the premiere, I came up with something a little special for Izzy and me. It's not going to cost you a penny and you're just going to love it!

STEPHEN. As long as you and Izzy are happy, I'm happy.

DOLLY. Wonderful! *(She heads back to her dressing room.)*

STEPHEN. Wait! – You did discuss whatever this is with Isobel, didn't you?

DOLLY. And spoil the surprise?

STEPHEN. But – you know she doesn't want to wear a costume!

DOLLY. She won't have a choice. While she was in the shower, I swiped her clothes...Have a great show, darling!

STEPHEN. Ma...

(But she's gone. The stage lights flicker.)

God...Lenny! The lights! Mr. Patterson? Sorry...what? Rehearsal? Oh, yeah, rehearsal went great...

ISOBEL. *(roaring from offstage)* Stephen!!!

STEPHEN. Hold on again...what is it, Izzy?

ISOBEL. *(emerging from her dressing room, also in a dressing gown)* Where the hell are my clothes?

STEPHEN. Uh...I understand that you have been given some kind of costume.

ISOBEL. I thought we decided, no costumes!

STEPHEN. Uh...

ISOBEL. I thought so. Have you seen what she has arranged for me?

STEPHEN. No, but it can't be that bad, can it? Look, we're fifteen seconds from air! ...Just deal with it for today and we'll fix it before next week, okay?

ISOBEL. I'll fix it all right... *(back to dressing room and slams door)*

STEPHEN. Okay, Mr. Patterson, we're ready to go! Yes, I'm sure you won't be disappointed! Goodbye, sir...okay! In five, four, three, two...

*(There is a pre-recorded drum roll, then **STEPHEN** announces:)*

Your Community Service Station, Cable Access Four, is proud to present the premiere broadcast of...*The Kitchen Witches!*

(The jingle continues.)

STEPHEN. *(cont.) Let's turn up the heat and bring this show to a boil*

With two ladies who mix as well as water and oil!

You never can tell what they'll be cooking up next

Someone could get hexed! They're sure to get vexed!

You could see a trick today, you could get a treat…

But chances are not only eggs and cream will be beat!

Now here is the twosome who'll keep you in stitches

It's Isobel and Dolly…The Kitchen Witches!

*(**DOLLY** enters, in green velvet Scarlett O'Hara "curtains" hoop skirt.)*

DOLLY. Well, I declare, ain't this just the prettiest audience I've evah seen! Welcome, deah friends to our new show. Today we'll be doin' our salute to the old South, an' cookin' up some mighty tasty vittles, like Burnin' of Atlanta Spare Ribs, Southern Fried Chicken Tara and somethin' that I like to call Rhett Butler Ham Steak! But you know – I seem to be missin' something…of course, of course! My deah friend and cooking partner! Dahlin', come on out now, the people are just dyin' to see you!

*(Izzy's dressing room door flies open and **ISOBEL**, dressed as Mammy [but no blackface!!], emerges. She is not happy. Not happy at all. There is a long, long moment in which **STEPHEN** tosses his script into a garbage can.)*

DOLLY. Well, I declare! It's Mammy! Come on over and say hello to the folks, Mammy!

ISOBEL. Why don't you go take a flying f…iddle dee-dee.

STEPHEN. We are gonna be so sued…

DOLLY. Now, of course, no salute to Southern Cookin' would be complete without Mammy's famous Buttermilk Biscuits. She makes them so good you'll think you've just died and gone to heaven!

ISOBEL. Somebody gonna die and go to straight to hell…

DOLLY. Ain't you funny, Mammy! Look, I'll get you started. Mix together two cups of flour with a tablespoon of sugar and a pinch of salt…

ISOBEL. Oh, give me that bowl – you don't know nothin' about birthin' no biscuits! And that's the sugar, this is the salt! I told you you'd mix them up, you ninny... oh, go over there and start the chicken and ribs! *(She tries to regain her composure and make the best of things.)* Hello, everyone! Now, it is true that I make the lightest, fluffiest buttermilk biscuits you've ever tried. And now you can make them at home too! It's a mighty sticky dough, so make sure you remove valuable jewelry before you start.

(ISOBEL *takes her heirloom ring off and puts it to the side.)*

Now. You just take a half cup of shortening...

ISOBEL.	**DOLLY.**
...cut into tiny little bits...	Mama's little baby loves shortnin', shortnin'...
...and rub it well into the flour mixture...	Mama's little baby loves shortenin' bread!
...adding a cup of buttermilk...	Mama's little baby loves shortnin', shortnin'...
...until you have a sticky mass of dough...	Mama's little baby loves shortenin' bread!
	(full volume) Put on the skillet!
...will you please *shut up!!!*	*Put* on the lid!...

DOLLY. Well! Wait 'til I tell Rhett about this!

ISOBEL. Frankly, my dear, I don't give a damn!!

DOLLY. *(turning away)* Hmph!

ISOBEL. Now. You turn the dough out onto a floured board and knead it, adding more flour as necessary.

DOLLY. While Mammy kneads her dough, I'll start our Burnin' of Atlanta Spare Ribs! For your marinade, you'll need 1 cup of dark blackstrap molasses, one cup of light soy sauce, 4 cloves of garlic and of course, what southern recipe would be complete without one whole cup of Kentucky Bourbon!

(She pulls out a flask from under her costume.)

You should always marinade your ribs for at least 12 hours. And marinade yourself for at least three!

(She takes a good nip as **STEPHEN** *once again sneaks behind the counter.)*

Woo! Now let's see how Mammy's biscuits are coming along... *(She sticks her fingers into the dough and eats a hunk.)* Mmm!

ISOBEL. Now, you know that eating raw dough is not good for you!

DOLLY. Who said?

ISOBEL. Honestly, you have no respect...Stephen, what are you doing down there?

STEPHEN. *(popping up from behind the counter with the bourbon flask)* Uh...

DOLLY. He's trying to steal my marinade fixin's. Ma dahlin' boy doesn't like me havin' a little tipple now and again...

ISOBEL. A *little* tipple? You go through more booze than a Dean Martin revival party!

DOLLY. Well, I nevah! I'll thank you to keep a civil tongue in your head and get back to your biscuits, Mammy!

(She smacks **ISOBEL** *with her fan.)*

ISOBEL. To hell with the biscuits! I am *not* your Mammy and I *refuse* to continue this ridiculous charade!

STEPHEN. *(back at his podium)* Isobel...

ISOBEL. Stephen, I did not study at the Cordon Bleu for four years just to end up on a tacky show, wearing an offensive costume and being made a fool of by some overstuffed Atlanta belle!

DOLLY. *(whisking her marinade)* Who are you calling overstuffed?

ISOBEL. Honey, we could fill you with helium and rename you Zeppelin!

DOLLY. Stephen, are you going to allow her to talk to your mother like that?

STEPHEN. Uh…

ISOBEL. Oh, save your breath, Stephen! It's time we admitted that this was a bad idea from the beginning! We were fools to think it could ever work. *(to camera)* Sorry, to disappoint you folks, but this show has just been cancelled!

(She begins to put her rings and watch back on.)

STEPHEN. Isobel, wait…

ISOBEL. There's nothing to wait for, Stephen, I'm through…All right, what did you do with it?

DOLLY. What?

ISOBEL. You know perfectly well what.

DOLLY. I declare, ah have no idea what you're talking about!

ISOBEL. My ring. It's gone.

DOLLY. You don't say.

ISOBEL. Give it back.

DOLLY. I cannot give back that which I do not have.

(She stirs her thick marinade.)

ISOBEL. I said - give it to me!!

DOLLY. All right!!

(With a spatula, she paints the marinade on ISOBEL's face. After a slow take to the audience, ISOBEL picks up the dough and stuffs it down the front of DOLLY's dress.)

DOLLY. Stephen!

STEPHEN. Isobel…

ISOBEL. I suppose you're going to take her side! Favouritism again!!

DOLLY. He's supposed to favour me! I'm his mother!

ISOBEL. Well, you just adopted him – I gave birth to him!

(STEPHEN spits out the mouthful of water he's been sipping. A take, then:)

STEPHEN. We'll be back right after this message from our sponsor… *(fade to….)*

(blackout)

ACT TWO

(The main curtain opens to reveal the set, which is much more "dressed up" than before. It is one week later. The counter unit is now split in two, with DOLLY's side on stage left and IZZY's on stage right. In between the two counter units, there is a small café table and two chairs.)

STEPHEN. *(looking extremely frazzled and fed up)* Hi everyone. I'm really glad so many of you showed up today, but I do have to let you know that due to our fire regulations, no-one can stand in the aisles. Basically, if you don't have a seat, you can't watch the show. Sorry… but hey! We turned away over a hundred people for today's broadcast, so count yourselves lucky! Mrs. H., let George sit beside you…I can't help it if he smells like mothballs. Deal with it. Now – I know that most of you are here because, a couple of weeks ago, I found out that I have a birth mother called Isobel, a real mom called Dolly, a dad named Larry who adopted me knowing he really was my dad but kept it a secret from Dolly and me until Isobel decided blurt it out on live TV, and now the show is a huge hit and my life is the main topic of discussion around every water cooler within broadcast range, which makes me very, very happy.

(ROB sticks a nicotine patch on STEPHEN then holds up one finger…)

That's one minute to air. Excuse me, folks – be right back… *(He crosses to the dressing room door and knocks.)* One minute, Ma! *(He immediately crosses to the opposite room.)*

DOLLY. *(offstage)* All right, Stephen darling!

STEPHEN. *(knocking on opposite door)* One minute…Ma.

ISOBEL. *(offstage)* Thank you, sweetheart!

STEPHEN. *(putting on headset at podium)* So...watch the sign and when it lights up, applaud or cheer or... do whatever the hell you want... In five...four...three...two... cue music!

(The jingle plays; during the instrumental break, **STEPHEN** *reads:)*

Today's sponsors are the Stirling Creamery, Center Lane Cadillac and Le Maison de Beouf, where you'll never get a bum steer.

(At the end of the jingle, the two **LADIES** *enter, dressed as glamorous witches in shiny cloaks.)*

BOTH. A witchy welcome to one and all!

(They cackle.)

ISOBEL. Hello, Mrs. H.!

DOLLY. Hello, Georgie!

BOTH. Hello Elm Street United Ladies Bridge Club!

ISOBEL. We have a terrific show for you today, folks...

DOLLY. It's Kitchen Witches Quickies Day!

ISOBEL. This is our own version of the Iron Chef challenge, where we have to come up with interesting ways to use the surprise ingredients Stephen has selected.

DOLLY. *(bursting with excitement)* But in our version, we have to come up with as many recipes as possible in *two minutes or less!* Isn't that a riot?

ISOBEL. But before we begin, I just want to say a special hello to Mr. Hugh Patterson, my favourite fan!

DOLLY. So you're hob-nobbing with Hugh Patterson now, are you?

ISOBEL. Well, we share so many of the same interests, belong to the same class of people, you know....

DOLLY. That's not what he said last night.

ISOBEL. What?

DOLLY. Last night, we had dinner at La Maison de Beouf... what a delightful man! And such excellent prime rib, and Yorkshire pudding to die for...

ISOBEL. If you think you can schmooze Hugh Patterson behind my back...

DOLLY. Schmooze? You think I'm schmoozing? I know you're trying to get your own show again, which is fine with me, I never want to see your face again... *(etc.)*

ISOBEL. ...You've got another think coming! I know perfectly well you're trying to get me kicked off this show and have your own program again... *(etc.)*

STEPHEN. Ladies!?

(They both stop.)

Viewer mail?

ISOBEL. *(instantly cheery again)* Oh! Is it viewer mail time already?

DOLLY. Time goes so quickly on the show, doesn't it? All right. Before we start our Kitchen Quickies, let's check our cauldron for viewer mail.

(With difficulty, they lift the huge cauldron from under the counter.)

ISOBEL. Ready?

DOLLY. Ready.

BOTH. Hubble bubble, snow and hail

Show us lots of witchy mail!

Toil and trouble, hail and snow,

Tell us what you want to know!

One, two...three!

(They each pull out a letter.)

DOLLY. Would you like to go first today, Izzy dear?

ISOBEL. No, dear – after you.

DOLLY. All right. This is a letter from Lucy from out on County Road Five. She writes, "Dear Kitchen Witches, You have so many interesting recipes - are there any plans for a cookbook? Yours witchily, Lucy M."

ISOBEL. If great minds don't think alike!

DOLLY. Lucy, we have wonderful news for you. We have just signed on with Edibles Publishing, and the Kitchen Witches Cookbook is going to be available everywhere by Thanksgiving!

ISOBEL. We are *so* excited! The hardest part, of course, is deciding which recipes to include.

DOLLY. And which photos.

ISOBEL. Photos?

DOLLY. Well, we have to have photos of us in it, don't we?

ISOBEL. Oh! You mean, of us posing with the completed dishes.

DOLLY. Well, that too, but I thought it would be more interesting if we included family photos! You know, of Stephen growing up and everything. People seem to be interested in that.

STEPHEN. Ma...

ISOBEL. You want to put family snapshots in our cookbook?

DOLLY. Sure!

ISOBEL. But then there would be no pictures of me.

DOLLY. *(all innocence)* Oh, I never thought of that.

ISOBEL. Ha! You know perfectly well I wasn't around when Stephen was growing up.

DOLLY. And whose fault is that?

STEPHEN. Ma...

ISOBEL. I thought we agreed not to discuss this on the air.

DOLLY. Discuss what? You *abandoning* your child?

ISOBEL. I did not abandon...I forbid you to talk about that!

DOLLY. I'm not talking about it – you are!

ISOBEL. You started it with the family snapshots! Listen, you wouldn't have a family at all if it weren't for me, Julia Childless!

DOLLY. How dare you...Ooo! *(DOLLY suddenly winces in pain and holds her stomach.)*

ISOBEL. What's the matter with you?

DOLLY. Oh, nothing. I just had too much prime rib last night... my tummy's a little unsettled...

ISOBEL. Great. I'm working with Emeril LeGassy.

DOLLY. It'll pass in a minute.

ISOBEL. Well, don't pass it over here!

DOLLY. You know, if I didn't have to walk so far from my dressing room…

ISOBEL. Don't you dare complain to me. You know I always arrive first, so it's only right…

STEPHEN. Alright!!… Sorry… *(through clenched teeth)* Get on with it…

ISOBEL. We can discuss the cookbook later.

DOLLY. You bet your ass…paragus we will.

STEPHEN. Letter number two!

ISOBEL. Letter number two is from Jane from Belleville.

DOLLY. Oh, hello, Jane! So nice to hear from you again!

ISOBEL. "Dear Witches, First of all, I'd like to thank Isobel for sending me her Steak and Kidney Pie recipe. I made it for a pot luck supper the other night, and everyone raved about it."

*(She looks up at **DOLLY**.)*

Oh, isn't that nice!

*(**DOLLY** "gags".)*

"But the real reason I'm writing is to let Stephen know that I have been a reformed smoker for 18 months now. I thought I'd never quit, but I was fortunate to have good friends who encouraged me and helped me through the worst of it. Please let Stephen know that if he needs a friend, he can give me a call any time, day or night. Love, Jane"

DOLLY. And look – she's listed her home phone, work phone, cell phone, fax number and e-mail address. Isn't that sweet?

ISOBEL. *(crossing to **STEPHEN**)* Here, Stephen dear. You keep this somewhere handy.

STEPHEN. Oh, I really don't think…

DOLLY. You know what they say - you can never have too many friends!

STEPHEN. But you can have way too many mothers!

ISOBEL. Say thank you to Jane for her nice letter, dear.

STEPHEN. *(into camera)* Thank you, Jane.

ISOBEL. And you'll give her a call sometime?

STEPHEN. I'll think about it. Let's get cooking now, okay?

BOTH. Witches? Prepare!

(Music as **DOLLY** *and* **ISOBEL** *take off their cloaks. Over their regular clothes, they are wearing matching aprons with witch silhouettes on the bibs.)*

DOLLY. Remember the Witch's rule, girls – before you work with food, you wash your hands and remove all your jewelry.

ISOBEL. And always be sure to put your jewelry somewhere safe so it won't be a temptation to someone who has no self-control whatsoever.

DOLLY. Isobel, get over it! For the last time, I didn't take your stupid ring...

ISOBEL. And I know you did...

DOLLY. And I know I didn't!

ISOBEL. Oh, you shoot more bull than Canada Packers!

DOLLY. Oh, I see. Now I'm not only a thief, I'm also a bull-shooter!

ISOBEL. You said it, I didn't.

(They are now nose-to-nose at centerstage.)

DOLLY. I've had about enough of you calling me a...ah! *(Her stomach pangs again.)*

STEPHEN. Ma?

ISOBEL. Don't get too close. The woman is powered by methane.

DOLLY. This is all your fault!

ISOBEL. *My* fault?

DOLLY. You've probably given me an ulcer.

ISOBEL. Nonsense! If you didn't snack constantly, you wouldn't have all these digestive upsets!

STEPHEN. Isobel, please! Are you all right to continue, Ma?

DOLLY. Of course! Just tell her to keep a civil tongue in her head.

STEPHEN. All right - it's time to invite our special guest up onto the stage for our Kitchen Witches Quickies segment!

ISOBEL. Wonderful!

DOLLY. Oh, this is going to be fun!

ISOBEL. You know, folks, we can't have a cooking contest without someone to decide the winner!

DOLLY. Stephen – do you have the name of today's celebrity judge?

STEPHEN. I do indeed! Would you please come up and join us in the kitchen…Mr. _____! *(name of a male audience patron. The name should be selected before each show.)*

(Theme music plays and the ladies ad lib until we get the male judge up on the stage and standing between the ladies.)

DOLLY. Well, hello! I'm Dolly Biddle…

ISOBEL. And I'm Isobel Lomax – call me Izzy.

DOLLY. So what do you do for a living?

(response)

ISOBEL. Tell me, dear, are you married?

(response…etc.)

DOLLY. Do you have any food allergies?

(Just in case the judge says yes, have a contingency plan!)

(in case of jacket or coat) Now, let me just get rid of this jacket, dear, you look so warm.

ISOBEL. And just in case things get messy, I think you should have some protection. Here, let me put it on...

*(**ISOBEL** helps him on with a waterproof cape.)*

DOLLY/ISOBEL. *(ad lib)* Now, you sit right down here, dear. *(They sit the victim at the café table.)* Comfy?

STEPHEN. *(when the judge is settled:)* I will now reveal today's Kitchen Witches Quickies challenge…In two minutes or less, you must make as many dishes as you can using items all related to…our favourite dinner course…dessert!

DOLLY. Ooo! Yummy!

ISOBEL. Excellent!

STEPHEN. Are you ready, witch Dolly?

DOLLY. Ready!

STEPHEN. Ready, witch Izzy?

ISOBEL. Ready!

STEPHEN. Ready celebrity judge? *(ad lib depending on response)*

Then upon your mark… get set… go!

*(Fast music plays as **STEPHEN** narrates and the ladies start rushing around the set.)*

*(Director's Notes: **STEPHEN**'s dialogue is ad libbed, depending on what happens on stage…but this segment works best if the ladies make the Judge stir, mix, whip with a hand mixer etc., and if there are lots of collisions and whipped cream accidents…the Judge can also get **DOLLY**'s secret stash of bourbon! The ladies must battle each other for ingredients and the judge's attention.)*

(Use whatever quickie recipes you want, as long as there's lots of whipped cream to play with!)

STEPHEN. And it's a race to the fridge…Dolly gets there a shade ahead of Isobel…they're being aggressive, two ladies who really know what they want…And back to the counters…it's Dairy for Dolly with a bowl of softened cream cheese, a quarter-cup of sour cream and the pitcher of milk while Isobel has secured a bowl of strawberries, some orange juice and…oh, yes! A full cup of delicious whipping cream! It's going to be interesting to see where that goes!

And they're off to the cupboards…what treasures will they find there and what wickedly delicious treats are these witchy minds conjuring up? Dolly has crushed vanilla wafers...some strawberry jam...Isobel is putting...let's see...cocoa powder, brown sugar and white sugar in a saucepan...wait a minute! Dolly has taken the orange juice from Isobel's counter!

(Blows a referee's whistle. The music stops.)

STEPHEN. A one-ingredient foul! Isobel ponders...what will she take from Dolly's side...the milk! She has taken the milk and is adding it to the dry ingredients in the saucepan! Dolly is not pleased with that, she may have to change some plans...and...resume cooking!

(music continues)

(Finally, the music ends with the ladies having finished three different creations each.)

Now, let's have our ladies describe what they've created for our celebrity judge! Dolly!

DOLLY. First, my summer-sweet Fruit Tarts, followed by my exotic Mexican-inspired dessert Tacos and of course, some melt-in your mouth Bourbon Balls!

STEPHEN. Isobel?

ISOBEL. Sweets for the sweet! I have a classic strawberry shortcake, yummy coconut macaroons and for the kids, Flipz and Dips!

STEPHEN. Celebrity judge, you have ten seconds to pick your winner. You must judge on appearance, variety, colour and of course, taste!

*("Timer" music as **DOLLY** and **ISOBEL** "help" the judge to taste their creations – in other words, force-feed him.)*

And now, it's time for our judge's decision. You cannot pick both ladies - just one! So who will it be, celebrity judge?

(ad lib depending on Judge's response)

DOLLY/ ISOBEL. *(whoever the Judge picks as the winner)* Thank you so much!

STEPHEN. *(hands winner an envelope)* And here is your prize package, which includes a one-night stay at The Bide-A-Wee Inn and dinner for two at La Maison de Boeuf…

ALL. Where you never get a bum steer!

(Ad-lib as the judge is returned to his seat to much applause.)

STEPHEN. Now we're just going to take a quick break for our Community Service announcements, then back for the wrap-up of today's show!

DOLLY. Don't change that channel!

BOTH. See you in a witchy minute!

(They cackle.)

STEPHEN. And…we're clear!

*(**DOLLY** makes another moan of pain.)*

ISOBEL. Oh, will you stop being such a drama queen!

STEPHEN. Ma, there's enough Gas-X, Pepto-Bismol and Tums in your dressing room to settle a Mexican bean eating contest. Go take something – I'll come get you before we go back live.

DOLLY. Oh, all right. But don't start without me - I'll be right back.

*(She makes a bee-line for the closest dressing room, which just happens to be **ISOBEL**'s.)*

ISOBEL. Hey! That's my dressing room…!

*(Too late – **DOLLY** slams her door.)*

Great. Now we'll have to get it fumigated.

*(**ISOBEL**, **ROB** and **STEPHEN** start cleaning up the set.)*

ISOBEL. I think Kitchen Quickies is going to be a great regular feature on the show, don't you?

STEPHEN. I guess.

ISOBEL. I thought it went really well today.

STEPHEN. Sure did.

ISOBEL. Whew! Getting all that done in two minutes is no picnic, let me tell you. And with the music galloping along like that...It's a real adrenaline rush!

STEPHEN. Must be.

ISOBEL. Stephen, are you ever going to speak to me in full sentences?

STEPHEN. What?

ISOBEL. It's been weeks since...well, since I dropped my little bombshell, and we've never really talked about it.

STEPHEN. What is there to say?

ISOBEL. I would think you'd be curious about...

STEPHEN. About what happened thirty-odd years ago?

ISOBEL. Well...yes.

STEPHEN. Well, I'm not.

ISOBEL. I just thought...

STEPHEN. Isobel, I like you. You're an interesting lady. And I'm sure you had your reasons for...for doing what you did, but it's ancient history, and I'm totally fine with that.

ISOBEL. Really?

STEPHEN. Really.

ISOBEL. Okay...but if you ever change your mind...

*(**ROB** is signaling one minute.)*

STEPHEN. One minute, Izzy.

ISOBEL. Thanks.

STEPHEN. *(knocking on the dressing room door)* One minute, Ma! *(no response)* Ma? *(He knocks again, then opens the door and looks in.)* Isobel, call an ambulance.

ISOBEL. What's wrong?

STEPHEN. Just call an ambulance - *hurry!*

(He exits into the dressing room.)

ISOBEL. *(rushing to the wall phone)* Switchboard? Call an ambulance immediately...I don't know exactly – but something's happened to Dolly!

(**ISOBEL** *rushes into the dressing room as well, leaving* **ROB** *alone with the audience. Realizing his camera is once again going live, he counts himself down, steps in front of it and waves to the home audience as we fade to…*)

(Blackout)

SCENE 2

(Dim lights come up on the kitchen set. It is deserted. Then **ISOBEL** *enters. She flicks on the overhead lights then stops for a moment, unsure of what she wants to do next. Then she takes an apron out of her bag, puts it on and starts cleaning the counters. A moment later,* **STEPHEN** *enters.)*

STEPHEN. Isobel?

ISOBEL. Oh! Stephen! I was just...I thought the place needed a bit of tidying up.

STEPHEN. The cleaning crew will do that in the morning, you know.

ISOBEL. I know, but I couldn't sleep. Might as well make myself useful.

STEPHEN. Okay. *(He starts to leave.)*

ISOBEL. You?

STEPHEN. *(turning back)* What?

ISOBEL. What are you doing here?

STEPHEN. There are only so many corridors in a hospital. Once you've walked them all about a hundred times you start getting dizzy. And that hospital smell...

ISOBEL. Yes. *(pause)* Do they know anything?

STEPHEN. They're not sure. They just told me to go home, get some rest, come back in the morning.

ISOBEL. That's probably best.

STEPHEN. Oh, yeah – rest. Right.

ISOBEL. You know, I bet you haven't eaten a bite all day. What you need is a good nourishing meal. *(She starts rummaging in the fridge...)*

STEPHEN. I'm not hungry.

ISOBEL. Maybe not, but it'll give us something to do.

STEPHEN. Really, I don't need you to fuss...

ISOBEL. What fuss? I'll just throw a few things together, then we can sit and have a nice chat and...

STEPHEN. Will you stop trying to mother me!

ISOBEL. Is that what you think I'm doing?

STEPHEN. Aren't you?

ISOBEL. Right now, all I'm trying to do is make you a sandwich.

STEPHEN. You've been trying to get close to me ever since you showed up here, but it's not going to work. Isobel - I already have a mother.

ISOBEL. *(sharply)* I know that! I chose her to be your mother. And I chose her because I knew that Dolly Biddle could raise you better than I ever could! Dolly was my best friend, you know.

(**STEPHEN** *looks quizzically at her.*)

Didn't know that, did you! Yep, we were as close as sisters, Dolly and I, all the time we were growing up in good old Sudbury. We spent every second together – sat next to each other in school, talked for hours on the phone, had sleep-overs…We were the first ones to wear dog collars on our ankles.

STEPHEN. Dog collars…?

ISOBEL. Left if you were going steady, right if you were available. Oh, we were quite the pair! Sourdough or rye?

STEPHEN. Uh…rye…

(*Through this section, **ISOBEL** assembles a sandwich for **STEPHEN**. They eventually end up at the café table, **STEPHEN** eating and listening.*)

ISOBEL. Our last year of high school, we met Larry Biddle. What a character! I remember the first day he drove into the school parking lot in his ancient wreck of a Ford Coupe. He taught your mother how to drive in that car.

STEPHEN. Really? Ma's a terrible driver.

ISOBEL. No kidding. She kept missing the clutch and stepping on the brake, stalled at every red light when she managed to stop at all, and never could find third gear. I'd be hanging on in the back, and Larry would be beside her in the front saying, "Grab the knob, grab the knob!" She'd yell, "I can't, I'm trying to drive!" Mustard or mayo?

STEPHEN. Mustard.

ISOBEL. Then in the summer of '64, Larry suddenly proposed – to me! I was stunned – I didn't want to get married! I had been working and saving every penny so I could go to Paris and study at the Cordon Bleu! So I turned him down. Larry was hurt and angry, embarrassed…and the very next day he proposed to Dolly. She was over the moon, planning their Christmas wedding and flashing the world's tiniest diamond! So I didn't wait - I got on the next plane to Paris. *(She gives him the sandwich.)* A little ground pepper?

STEPHEN. Uh…okay.

ISOBEL. Three years later, I'm returning in triumph as a Chef of the Cordon Bleu! But Dolly was stuck in Sudbury, slinging hash in a diner. Before long, Larry and I met up again in Toronto and there we were, just two hormone-driven teenagers again…Oh, I'm sorry - I've said too much…

STEPHEN. No – I just need something to go with this sandwich. And if I know my mother… *(He finds a mickey bottle in a decorative oven mitt.)* Thought so. *(takes a swig)* Okay, let me guess - three months later…

ISOBEL. Three months later, I had a Biddle bun in my oven. What a mess – Dolly desperately wanted children, but couldn't have them. I didn't want kids but found I could pop them out like toaster strudels. So we quietly arranged it with an adoption agency and the day after you were born, you became part of the Biddle family, and I started up the career ladder.

STEPHEN. And forgot about me.

ISOBEL. *Forget* you? I thought of you every single day. Every time Larry came down to Toronto he'd bring photos of you, report cards, and…look. *(She opens her purse and takes out a small box.)*

STEPHEN. What's that?

ISOBEL. A lock of your hair. Two of your baby teeth.

STEPHEN. There's something you don't see every day.

ISOBEL. Well, you know the rest of the story. During one of Larry's Toronto trips, he had that heart attack in the motel and next thing I know, I'm at his funeral, hiding in the back row. Of course, your mother saw me…apparently, that was the first time a funeral was reported in the sports section.

STEPHEN. Wow. My life is a soap opera.

ISOBEL. Your life has been filled with people who love you…one way or another. It may have been a little unconventional but - not so terrible, really. Was it?

STEPHEN. No - it wasn't terrible. Life with Ma has always been pretty darn interesting.

ISOBEL. Like I said – I always knew Dolly would a better mother to you than I ever could be. And believe me, Stephen - I know I'll never replace her in your heart. No-one ever could. But if I could fit into your life *somewhere*…well, that would be a greater gift than I could ever deserve.

STEPHEN. Isobel – I'm gonna need a little more time…

ISOBEL. You take as much time as you want. You're gonna be okay, kiddo. And you know what? Dolly's gonna be okay too. I know it. Now. How about some coffee and dessert. I think we still have some of those pastry shells…

STEPHEN. *(grabbing her hand as she stands)* Isobel?

ISOBEL. Hmm?

STEPHEN. Thanks.

(**ISOBEL** *gently touches his cheek and they share a smile. Then she starts assembling dessert as we fade to…*)

(Blackout)

SCENE THREE

(One week later – the next Kitchen Witches broadcast.)

STEPHEN. *(done as a taped voice over)* Ladies and gentlemen! Your Community Service Station, Cable Access Four, is pleased to present the number one cooking show on the community dial...The Kitchen Witches!

(The jingle plays. At the end of the music, on the regular cue, **ISOBEL** *enters from her dressing room in her fancy witch's cloak and hat.)*

ISOBEL. A witchy welcome to one and all! *(cackles)* Now, you regular viewers will notice that we seem to be one witch shy of a coven today! Yes, last week my co-host Dolly Biddle was taken seriously ill, ended up in the hospital, poor thing. But you know the famous saying – the show must go on - right, Stephen? *(She takes off her hat and cloak.)*

STEPHEN. Right you are, Isobel! Today's show is sponsored by the Stirling Creamery and Frank's Café and Service Station – Eat Lunch and Get Gas.

ISOBEL. And today's theme is Goodies from your Garden! *(She takes a large basket of greens from under the counter.)* We're going to start today by making a lovely julienne salad with low-fat dressing and my special herbed croutons. You know, if our friend Dolly had eaten more fruits and veggies instead of nibbling on all those fatty foods, she'd be up and around right now, saying...

DOLLY. *(slamming open the studio door and entering)* All right! That's about as much as I can take.

ISOBEL. Why, Dolly Biddle! You're supposed to be at home, resting!

DOLLY. That's what you'd like, isn't it, you hag from hell! Me at home on my deathbed, gasping my last breath, while you happily decapitate veggies and plot to take over the show!

ISOBEL. Well, it wouldn't be right to disappoint my loyal viewers, would it?

DOLLY. Oh, by the way - is this your knife? It's the one I just pulled from my back!

STEPHEN. Ma…

DOLLY. And you! I expected as much from her, Stephen, but I never expected that you would turn against your own mother! Your *real* mother!

STEPHEN. Ma, if you'd just be quiet and listen for one minute…

ISOBEL. Stephen and I have something to say to you…

DOLLY. Oh, it's "Stephen and I" all of a sudden! Well, isn't that enough to make you hurl…

STEPHEN. Cue music!

(*A music intro plays – possibly "*Hello Dolly*", or if rights to that song cannot be arranged, use any upbeat music. **DOLLY** gets a huge bouquet, and is outfitted with a tiara and red velvet cape and promenaded around the set – Queen Dolly! If budget allows, balloons can fall from the ceiling, etc.*)

DOLLY. My! I don't know what to say!

ISOBEL. Surprised?

STEPHEN. It was Isobel's idea, Ma.

DOLLY. *Her* idea?

STEPHEN. Yeah. She wanted to give you a big welcome back!

ISOBEL. How are you feeling, Dolly? I'm sure your fans at home want to know just as much as we do.

DOLLY. Well – I feel fine. A little weak at the knees, but glad to be back. And thank you so much for all the cards and letters and flowers, folks. That nice young male nurse was kept really busy finding space for them all. (*to* **ISOBEL**) You know, he flirted outrageously with me…that is, until I threw up on his shoes.

ISOBEL. I can see how that would put a damper on things.

DOLLY. It turns out it was nothing serious, folks - just a big old clump of stuff that got stuck on the way out. One industrial-size enema and – *(raspberry sound)* - here I am, good as new and about five pounds lighter! I tell you, it was like trying to pass a bowling ball!

ISOBEL. *(laughing)* Oh, Dolly - it's good to have you back!

DOLLY. I must say - it's wonderful to see you laugh again, Izzy.

ISOBEL. Oh, Dolly - I've missed you! And - I want to tell you how sorry I am about Larry…I should have said it long ago. What a terrible, terrible thing to do to a friend…

DOLLY. *You're* sorry? How about me? Marrying the poor man purely for spite!

ISOBEL. I've wanted to clear the air for so many years….

DOLLY. Me too…oh! And if we're confessing our sins…

ISOBEL. Mmm?

*(**DOLLY** takes the ring from her pocket.)*

My ring! Dolly! You did have it all along!

DOLLY. I sure did. Of course, I didn't *know* I had it.

ISOBEL. What?

DOLLY. Remember that big glop of buttermilk biscuit dough I ate a few weeks back?

ISOBEL. Yes.

DOLLY. I thought it was awfully lumpy.

ISOBEL. You mean, you…*(She points at **DOLLY**'s stomach.)*

DOLLY. Caused a backup worse that the 401 at rush-hour. Doc said it's one of the more unusual items he's seen go through.

ISOBEL. *(holding it far away from her)* You don't say.

DOLLY. You can keep it now.

ISOBEL. Gee, thanks. But you know, since it's a Biddle family heirloom, maybe it's time that I pass it - pardon the pun – to the next generation.

*(She crosses to the podium and gives it to **STEPHEN**.)*

Here, dear. Wear it in good health.

STEPHEN. Gee…thanks. *(He tucks it in a kleenex and puts it under the podium.)*

ISOBEL. You know, that ring sat in the bottom of my jewelry box for years. I only wore it on the show because I knew it bugged you! The whole thing seems so silly now, doesn't it.

DOLLY. But you know what's not silly?

ISOBEL. What?

DOLLY. Look! *(She holds up their creation.)* We've made a beautiful, hi-fiber, low-fat, mouth-watering julienne salad - big enough for a family…

*(taking **ISOBEL**'s hand and looking at **STEPHEN**)*

…of *three*.

ISOBEL. A family of three. Oh, I like that.

DOLLY. Stephen? Come and join us! You can be today's celebrity judge!

(They begin to set the café table.)

STEPHEN. You two go ahead – I have plans to eat after the show.

ISOBEL. You have a lunch date?

STEPHEN. No!

(They are staring at him.)

Well…maybe…

DOLLY. How exciting! With who?

STEPHEN. Oh, no-one you know.

ISOBEL. Who has he had time to meet?

DOLLY. That nice nurse from the hospital?

STEPHEN. No.

DOLLY. The check-out girl at the Super-Save?

STEPHEN. Who?

ISOBEL. Jane from Belleville!

STEPHEN. No! …No, it's not… Okay, yes, it is.

ISOBEL. I knew it! *(to the camera)* You *go*, Jane girl!

DOLLY. Isn't that wonderful!

(*They start to dish out the food.*)

Where are you taking her? Oh, I know... La Maison de Beouf...

ALL. Where you never get a bum steer!

STEPHEN. No, no. I'm going over to her place. She's cooking.

ISOBEL. What's she making?

STEPHEN. Well, I think she's going to....

DOLLY. Isobel – just think. If things work out, in a little while, we'll be planning our first grandchild!

STEPHEN. Ma...

DOLLY. You'll have to bring her flowers ...

STEPHEN. Okay...

ISOBEL. And wear just a hint of cologne...

STEPHEN. I will...

DOLLY. And most importantly...

ROB. Wash your hands, man.

(*The lights fade out during the following, which happens simultaneously.*)

ISOBEL. You know, I never had much of an urge to be a mother, but I sure like the idea of being a grandmother!

DOLLY. I can start putting up jars of baby food and you can knit some booties.

STEPHEN. Well, that's about all we have time for today, folks.

On behalf of our sponsors and your Community Service Station, Cable Access Four, this is Stephen Biddle, asking you to tune in next week, same Witch-time, same Witch-station.....

ISOBEL. Knit booties? Dolly Biddle, you know perfectly well that I hate to knit!

DOLLY. Well, someone has to knit the booties…

(He listens for a moment…)

ISOBEL. Besides, my baby food is approved by Health Canada…

DOLLY. That may be so, but I know what babies really like since I have had real experience…

ISOBEL. Oh, here we go. I knew you couldn't go two minutes without bringing that up one last time! *(etc.)*

Jane, I may be a little late.

(blackout)